Bio Marty Vita:
Life Life Life

Mike Spiritfair Marty
Get a JAHB, LLC

Paperback ISBN-13: 979-8-9868943-5-5

BIOGRAPHY & AUTOBIOGRAPHY / Personal Memoirs
BIOGRAPHY & AUTOBIOGRAPHY / Philosophers
BIOGRAPHY & AUTOBIOGRAPHY / Social Activists
BIOGRAPHY & AUTOBIOGRAPHY / Religious

Get a JAHB, LLC (Publisher)
Milwaukee, Wisconsin
USA

Dedicated to the Memories of William Tyndale,
Peter Schöffer the Younger,
and... June Marty

BORN

Mike Spiritfair Marty was born Michael Scott Marty in Iowa of the United States of America in 1967 Anno Domini. In China and Korea, as a newborn, he might have already been considered to be one year old. Marty's first airplane flight was from the Virgin Islands (St. Croix) to Miami, Florida when he was still one year old biologically, but these early details hopefully will never be misconstrued as a virgin newborn birth.

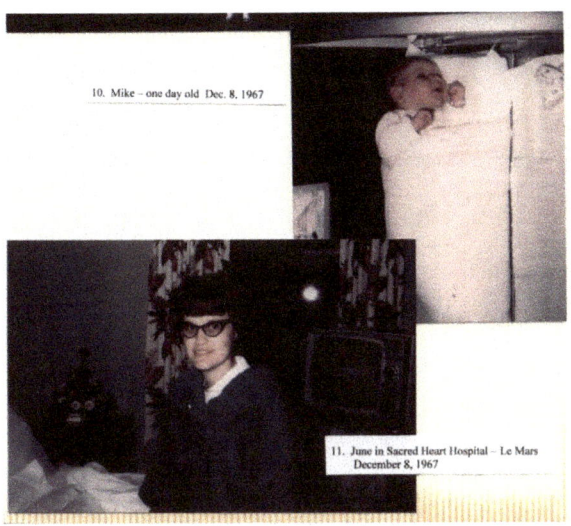

10. Mike – one day old Dec. 8, 1967

11. June in Sacred Heart Hospital – Le Mars
December 8, 1967

Swaddling clothes in Iowa

His mother, June, did a good job of interpolating friends for photo shoots, but more and more, year by year, Marty became convinced of, and reconciled with, his solitary nature[005].

6. Mike's 7th Birthday Dec. 1974

Friends in Iowa (bio age 7)

This pensive disposition might either have been intensified, or even have begun, during, and following, a 1978 school year in the Philippine Islands[011] where his father, Wayne, was teaching during a sabbatical year.

Philippine classmates (bio age 11)

A penchant for bizarre and extraordinary thinking and behavior might also have begun during, and following, Marty's 5th-grade faraway experience.

Philippine teachers and administrators

Marty's emotional exhilaration might have peaked pre-puberty[038], with his contemplative direction eventually becoming detrimental to finding his future career, sex, and general fit in American society with ease.

WORLD INTERACTIONS

Feelings

Marty had some typical, vast, straight lasciviousness appear as a young teenager, but he never considered these feelings and desires to be a central, critical, or fundamental, aspect of his identity[127].

Later, in 1992, he tried to assert some of his serious predilections upon others[025], with limited success. An overall lack of fulfillment and satisfaction gave rise to heartache[050], discontent[073], renunciation[056], and stoicism[071].

He tried, at times, to remind himself of the interconnection of the events in his life with his understanding of God through his mind and/or brain and/or mind and/or brain[030].

At times, he imagined he was capable of doing some good things for other people in his life[036]. This might have been imagined and not real.

Based on his life's total assortment of thoughts and events up until that point, on August 29th, 1991, he wrote, "I have no desire before I die to do anything except change the world for Jesus[015].

While living again in the hometown of his biological birth (in an apartment only five blocks away from the former hospital building), he would sometimes have altercations[106] with one, or with both, of his parents who lived on the other side of town.

Parents in a train car,
with Marty's 2nd-floor apartment
showing through the windowpane

Later, in 2010, during his MBA program, he wrote, "there are almost no restrictions or restraints or laws with respect to the most powerful power in the world-- the feeling of intercourse or ejaculation...[121]" This was a thought he had; a thought about a feeling.

In 1995, after watching a motion picture, he remarked about the feeling of art where observers can share an affinity with the "love and beauty and truth of the writer[072]."

The next year, he expressed a desire not "to describe the world as it is... [but] to describe how the kingdom of love should be[087]."

At age 8 (vita, or a few days before his 28th biological birthday), he wrote: "Don't give up, don't give in, Marty. Keep pushing the limits... one day I'll die and then I can stop trying[077]."

Failure

Not everything that Marty has done in his life has

been successful. That is obvious. On February 4th, 1996, he tried to have a serious talk with an acquaintance who was a teenage girl about the concept and idea of suicide, but there was not much mutual agreement, so the conversation just kind of ended hanging in the air[082].

Acclimatization to Evil ("Mental Health")

An argument can be made that Mike Spiritfair Marty is maladjusted on purpose. In the autumn of 2009 he made the realization that survival of the fittest means the survival of those most conducive to some particular task rather than the survival of those who are the healthiest or strongest[117]. To an extent, this means that those who are fittest are those who are the most adaptive or acclimatized.

On November 7th, 2010, Marty jotted down a one-page idea questioning whether "women's evolutionary judgment [results] in justice and peace and truth[129]." Christianity--in theory--cares about peace... truth... AND justice. Pragmatic "Christianity," on the other hand, only cares about "balance" (i.e. the "balance" sheet, profit and loss, retained earnings).

YouTube thumbnails (vita age 33)

Is addiction to money an illness? Marty thinks so. "Loving" and "selling" are so intertwined (Latin "venus")[113] that admitting this can be painful to those who are in denial. Perfect mental health does not include people who are in denial. Happy hedonism[053] can sometimes (always?) wear blinders.

On January 30th, 2000 Anno Domini, in the first month of the last year of the last millennium, Marty made an effort to distinguish former from contemporary, strict or vulgar, definitions of two abstract concepts: "the kingdom of God" and "God is in control[096]." These two concepts have played a substantial role in *Sex with Jesus*.

Marty believes he is not unreasonable to suggest that harmony (harmonious mental health, so called) within an evil system is neither good nor just[054].

Counter Culture

When he was 14 years old, Marty had a classmate die by suicide (April 1982). The next year, a former classmate died in a car crash (July 1983). A month later, Marty himself got hit by a Greyhound bus while illegitimately "borrowing" his friend's motor scooter (August 1983). Death and suicide did not become preoccupations in his life thenceforth, but he certainly was aware of these parts of life. Is death a part of life? It is.

On March 23rd, 1996, Marty noted an interesting description of suicide from Plato's *Phaedo*[086], and he also wrote that "the church... is a spiritual whorehouse where the members pay to be relieved at regular intervals from the burden of their meaningless lives[086]." This is an example of Marty's tendency to be less pragmatic and more counter-cultural. Perhaps <u>culture</u> loves comfort and ease while <u>counter-culture</u> needs (wants) the real and the true[074]. Perhaps <u>counter culture</u> asks questions[010] while <u>culture</u> ignores the questions that stare us all in the face.

A few years earlier (1993), Marty had amazed a teenage girl with his world-overthrowing convictions[034]. Marty has since acknowledged that overthrowing the world is a little more complicated, and it can take a little more time, than he had first anticipated.

After a decade or so, Marty was mostly able to work through his angry after-college, righteous-indignation phase[027]. These days, when he has righteous indignation, he tries to include himself among the people whom he blames for this, that, or the other thing.

Possibly, Marty's biggest counter-cultural movement is his general petition to outlaw the greeting, "How are you?" He considers this greeting to be a Jewish (Old Testament) greeting (cf Exodus 18:7, RSV), and people who are Jewish may use it freely. But Jews (who are only masquerading as Christians) annoy him because the greeting is not a Christian one, in his opinion[133]. There is no known Christian text that refers to asking about another's welfare, but there are many cases where Christians wish each other well. The distinction is not immaterial.

YouTube thumbnails (vita age 33)

Further, he rants:
You ask me how I am. Why don't you tell me? What if I'm doing well. Isn't it bragging if fortune is smiling kindly on me? 'Let another man praise you, and not your own mouth; A stranger, and not your own lips' (Proverbs 27:2). Am I kind? Am I boring? Am I cowardly? Am I beautiful? Do I give you pleasure? Do I make you uncomfortable? Do you like me? Do you love me? Am I sensitive to your moods, your joys, your pains? Am I unperceptive and cold? Why don't you tell me 'how I am' and how I make you feel. Unless I make no impression on you whatsoever, in which case you probably don't care about me at all, so why pretend that you do by asking 'how I am[099]'.

That same teenage girl whom he impressed in 1993 with his world-changing convictions, two months later asked if his plans would change, and he said, "No[041]." Even with little external reinforcement or encouragement, have they changed in the last three decades?; uh, maybe... "No."

In September 2000, Marty addressed some biblical philosophical questions[103] (inerrancy of the Bible, etc.) to a hometown M. Div. friend of his family, but only on paper. He didn't actually deliver the questions to the friend until sending a text on his friend's birthday 21 years later.

On December 3rd, 1997, Marty recorded "a vague idea" concerning the Gross National Product, mental health, birth rates, and suicide[094]. Overall, the idea relates to how society tries to keep suicidal people alive "against their will."

Parents' backyard (vita age 9, or thereabouts)

Another intuition (or thought) he had in 2000 revolved around death, individual death, God, and that "God is the possibility in this life[097]." The thought also related, perhaps, to the subtle transition over the centuries from Christianity being a monotheistic, existentialist religion to its current state largely of being a pantheistic religion.

It wasn't until 2010 when he realized that conservatives are anti-abortion for this reason: if poor people are allowed to have abortions, there wouldn't be enough slaves to support the capitalist economy in the future[122].

Part of Marty's counter-cultural attitude relates to honesty, the youngest of the virtues (per Nietzsche). He thinks that sexual honesty, actual, real, sexual honesty[109], is better for society in terms of reducing adverse selection. It's a theory. He's a 5-1/4" (L) and 4-3/4" (C)[120].

Active Efforts to Change World (in a Particular Direction)

Do people have to be utopians to try to make a better world[047] (or a new world)? Is the world perfect? Is there anything that can be improved? Is there anything that some people would prefer to the current world[061]? Only Pangloss says that this world is the best of all possible worlds. Many people aspire to talk like Pangloss, even though Pangloss is a clodpoll, is he not?

In 1990, on winter break from Iowa State University classes, Marty decided "to commit [him]self to being the best teacher of agape love in the world[014]." What is agape love? Presumably, this definition is part of what he committed himself to teach.

Cancer struck Marty in 1995. With a lot of help from people in his life, he recovered. Near the end of his six-month chemotherapy regimen, still uncertain about whether he had thus far taken any concrete steps to achieve his goals in life, he took one--a concrete step:

A policeman stopped and asked me where I was going at such a late hour (about 3 miles east of Le Mars) and I told him everything save giving him a copy of CRIES. Finally, he said, 'okay,' and I said 'thank you, sir,' and he drove off. Delivered 10 in Oyens--only a couple barking dogs. Then 39 in Remsen--a couple more barking dogs, but nothing major[069].

Another concrete step, literally--ouch, that must have hurt--was when he purposefully, but without proper forethought--stepped off of a moving Homecoming parade float and ripped a hole in a $200 rental tuxedo[003]. He was irked by some of the superficial general comments of his fellow "floaters." So he decided to do something about it. In retrospect, coming up with an alternative idea might have been wiser.

High school homecoming (bio age 17)

Plato says that pain and pleasure are often tied

together, and they follow one another in succession. The answer? Don't seek pleasure. Avoid pain. Create. Be excellent[090].

In 1989, during summer classes, he gave a speech on monitoring depression[009]. At the time, a friend of his was feeling a little low. This was an active effort on his part to understand.

Did Marty's first active attempts at changing the world in a particular direction happen in 1989[012], in 1991[018], earlier than that, or later than that? Maybe they haven't happened at all yet, other than wishful thinking. Maybe *Sex with Jesus* is Marty's first crazy/sane attempt with a chance to succeed.

HIS SEX WANTS

Oh, I got called in to work today at 11 and worked 11:30 to 7 and made 32 deliveries in the freezing rain and only fell twice. Including the fence I broke outside of our apartment yesterday, that makes 3. Norm says if he didn't know any better, he'd think I was in love. Well, I think I am. Without a doubt[021].

Being in love with a woman is, of course, different from being in love with the idea of (and the ideas attributed to) Jesus Christ, but apparently there are a few similarities.

After Iowa State University, and a couple years before his cancer ordeal, Marty consciously and "intentionally" masturbated and ejaculated for the first time, though it was a surprise and accidental[037]. This topic did not specifically get addressed as part of his cancer mental evaluation.

Marty's most exhaustive sexual self-analysis was compiled a week after this surprise experience, and it included references to Stacy Thoms, Jackie Gorrell, Laura Doorenbos, Marla, Melanie, Kathy Nutt, and Tanya as highlights, while not mentioning a handful of others who could have been included[038]. General synopsis? The cancer clinical analysis (above) might be the most reliable summation overall: "He has sublimated his desires and intellectualized his aggressive side, rationalizes his loneliness."

Parthenon ruins in Greece (bio age 11)

One time later that year, after work, Marty wrote, "Tammy asked me out. I fudged around it--she said she had a boyfriend, and I brought that up, and I told her I was a Jesus freak and that I really didn't have time for girls[043]."

In perhaps a related bio life/vita life notebook entry, on November 9th, 1994 (2-1/2 months before the first signs of cancer), Marty wrote, "I'm giving up on my family. Got two weak/frustrating letters from Lynnae and Alan and it's just not worth it. My family is the human race[060]."

A week later, he mentioned this renunciation to his mom, and he tried to explain a little, including "some of Jesus' statements on family[062]."

A year and a half later, after the family that he renounced had helped him to recover from his cancer (or would not let him die like he had wished), he wrote, "I am not happy. I had always hoped to get the girl, but now that seems quite beyond reach, and maybe not even wise[085]."

Two months later (on May 13th, 1996), he wrote, "I wish I could solve the girl question and the life question, but I haven't been able to yet, and it's frustrating[092]." Perhaps, it took him another 27 years.

On August 17th, 2000, Marty wrote:

The confusion over humanity's inborn nature, whether we are born good or bad, whether we are supposed to do 'what's natural' or resist our impulses, comes, in part, from verses like these: 'we once conducted ourselves in the lusts of our flesh, fulfilling the desires of the flesh and of the mind, and were by nature children of wrath' (Eph. 2:3); 'their women exchanged the natural use for what is against nature. Likewise also the men, leaving the natural use of the woman, burned in their lust for one another' (Rom. 1:26-7); 'His divine power has given to us all things that pertain to life and godliness... that through these you may be partakers of the divine nature, having escaped the corruption that is in the world through lust' (2 Pet. 1:3, 4). What is natural, what is given to us by nature, and are we to deviate (either 'rise above' or 'sink below') from this or 'obey' it? Yes, marriage. Is marriage natural? Are you sure? You can quote Matthew 19:6 if you want, but are you sure the meaning is crystal clear, and do you really believe it? But more than just marriage. Natural or unnatural? Gray. It depends. I'd like to talk about it[101].

Three weeks later, he contemplated whether, how, and to what extent, serving women and serving God was, is, and can be compatible (or not)[102].

As a precursor to *Sex with Jesus*, during the summer of 2007 (probably while he was taking either Principles of Financial Accounting or Business Statistics, with a scattering of gorgeous 19-year-old University of

Northern Iowa female students sitting around him, e.g. Erika and Vicki), he wrote, "I want to bring Jesus into my sex life but pretty women absolutely do not want Jesus to be in their sex life--so there is no connection nor even a possibility of one[107]."

Milwaukee apartment bathroom (vita age 24, bio age 44)

Later in the autumn of 2007, Marty had an epiphany about "sex, truth, money" and about how to integrate them. "Why Peace Is Bad--Is Truth Bad? Is "Ich Du" satisfying or superficial? If it's satisfying, is it antiprogressive?[112]"

Milwaukee living room (vita age 24, bio age 44)

In January 2009, he considered the possibility of talking about "the dark" and about his sex life--"searching for greater understanding"--with a University of Northern Iowa counselor--one hour a week. That didn't happen (except for one short introductory meeting)[115].

On August 3rd of that same year, Marty wondered, "Does science say that cross-fertilization is good and religions generally do not support this? Is this the primary conflict between science and religion?[116]"

Later, in 2013, he questioned, "the feeling I had and have that people do not want Jesus to have anything to do with their sex lives and the progression of the sexual righteousness surveys project (keep out!)? [that's not right. I haven't really done anything with the surveys yet including creating them, after the background material has been gathered...[132]"

DEATH WANTS

As mentioned in Marty's Counter-Culture World Interactions, death presented itself to him as early as at age 14. In addition to the 1983 car and bus crashes, the first death of one of Marty's grandparents had also happened earlier in March of that year.

Whereas a fifth to a quarter (or more) of teenagers think about the joy of being dead, Marty was one of them when he wrote, "If I had any guts what-so-ever, I would kill myself. I wish everyone would just leave me ALONE[004]." He echoed this thought a decade later on July 1st, 1994[055], and the next month on August 8th[057]. That same month, on the 22nd, he scribbled, "Came home and thought 'why should I live?' I don't enjoy it. Tried to write a suicide note but I'm not motivated enough[058/059]." Six months later, his first cancer pangs began. During the initial part of his cancer diagnosis, he also talked about his willingness to die. (Marty finally managed to pen his classic literature suicide note a dozen years later on September 21st, 2006.)

Somewhere on Earth, maybe in the Philippines when he was ten or eleven, Marty observed a painting (possibly this one) that was entitled "MARTYRDOM," which he mistakenly read as "Marty-room." This was presumably his first introduction to the concept of a martyr. The similarity of this word to his name has crept into his thinking in such a way that every so often he dreams of death as a martyr. Wrong or right, he believes that such a death is more noble and virtuous than either (1) suicide or (2) a slow death in a living/dying facility.

On December 9th, 1993, he wrote, "I've prayed like

this before--he didn't give me Kathy, he didn't let me go to New York and become our nation's spiritual leader (not yet). I prayed for several huge things that I hoped to accomplish before I martyred out at 37 or 38[045]."

On February 25th, 1996, he similarly wrote, "It's just not worth the effort. Life, that is. Amazing. I'm sorry but I'm just floored. Early death through martyrdom, I guess. I must not forget it. I guess this is just God helping me to remember[083]."

HIS SEX FULFILLMENTS

Marty's first kiss was in the early morning hours of April 14th, 1985[066], parked in a car in his parents' driveway. His first oral intercourse was with the same person, 3-1/2 months later[001], under the light switch, around the corner near the ping-pong table in the basement. (He started his high school daily journal record on this day, likely precipitated by this event.) This activity might have been repeated a second, a third, or a fourth time, but these (if real) are less remembered and not as well documented.

On the 30th anniversary of his girlfriend's parents' wedding, he almost had sex with her, but... he didn't[002]. Not many 17-year-old boys turn down opportunities to have sex with 18-year-old girls. This puts Marty in an extremely exclusive category. He didn't feel ready. He was maybe a little uncertain and scared. He maybe felt it was a life choice with a direction to which he wasn't ready to commit.

When Marty was living with his fraternity friend in an Ankeny apartment in 1991, he didn't sleep in a bed; he slept on the floor. When he moved back to his hometown six months later, he slept again in his high school bed until he decided on June 4th, 1993 that he was "gonna start sleeping on the floor[039]." This was five days subsequent to his first "intentional" accidental ejaculation event[037] mentioned previously. When he moved across town to his apartment in 1994, he slept again on the bed that was provided with his room. Eventually, he decided the room was too small to have a bed in it, so he got rid of it, and he transitioned once more to sleeping on the floor.

On May 19th, 1989, he wrote:

Golfed this afternoon at Homewood with Keno, Stu, and Krummen--shot a 56. Thought a lot about Kathy and Vicki today--Kathy left for California this morning. I told Keno I was sick of looking at girls after he told me to look at a couple of them. I've really got to figure out who I am this summer, my goals, and how I can achieve them. It was a fun day...[007]

That is the extent of Marty's sexual fulfillments. LOL. He kissed two women on the cheek (in 1979 and in 2003). (There was also a 1983 hometown spin-the-bottle birthday party where he probably kissed a couple of teenage girls on the cheek, but he can't recall their names.) There were also two women who each gave him a memorable cheek-to-cheek side hug which was almost close enough to be called a kiss... but not quite (in 1988 and in 1993).

Sometimes people murder each other. Life can be traumatic. If Marty had had none of these experiences, he might have been even angrier than he was during his angry period. Quien sabe. At least, for these few experiences, he can be thankful. Thanks, ladies.

Finally, as mentioned earlier in his epiphany note[112], the dichotomy between serving women and himself vs. serving something a little more ideological and truthful has played out in Marty's life by him choosing (or relenting to) the more ideological way... in which he "would like to be the national spiritual leader of [his] generation (and beyond)[067]" while confessing as needed about his 39-year-old person, University of Northern Iowa women-problem-solving stopgap measure[108]."

SELF-KNOWLEDGE

Who is Marty? LOL. On November 18th, 1989, he wrote, "... the conversation afterwards led me to think about my priorities again. <u>Did I place too much emphasis directly on God instead of focusing my God-given talents toward excellence while always focusing indirectly on God?</u> Is that compromising? I'll keep struggling[013]."

One of his first stabs at writing a literary query letter was on October 17th, 1991, when he wrote:

My name is Michael Scott Marty, I am 23 years old, and I am ready to die. I wouldn't mind living for another five or twenty or seventy years, I'd love to get married and raise some kids, I'd love to experience even more of the joys of life like family and friends and nature, but I'm not scared of death. My short time on earth has been complete. I've known success and I've lived through pain. I've experienced the ecstasy of being alive. I'm ready to leave this earth whenever that time might come[019].

This paragraph is still accurate, except the part about him living another "seventy years," and also his middle name has changed.

In 1991, he wrote, "Lord, I want to lead this generation[020]," and in 1993, he wrote, "Writing is my gift. I can do it. I can write the book and [the script]. It's hard, but it's the only creative outlet I know of for everything that's going on in my mind[040]."

One thing Marty certainly has not resolved yet is his wish, when he wrote, "And I thought how much I wanted to lead these youths out of pettiness and into a love of the truth which is a pure love for God and for all of mankind[024]."

Not sure if Marty had an advanced inkling of his 1995 cancer when, on December 13th, 1992, he wrote, "[T]hose two lumpy bumps on my left side really kind of bum me out. What are they? If they're cancer, what am I gonna do?... Maybe it's to constantly remind me of the physical pain of others so I can relate. I must press on[031]."

Just after Valentine's Day, 1993, Marty wrote, "You don't know what you can do until you try it. Until you push yourself beyond the limits of conventional acceptability. Whatever that is![033]"

A year later, Marty visited his former high school and discussed his life's desires with a former teacher. "Told him I wanted to be free and write the truth. I don't think he thought that was too weird[049]."

Later that same month, he wrote, "John 15:8. John 15:14--that's who I want my friends to be, those who seek to do Jesus' commands as I do[051]."

Marty acknowledged an as yet unsatisfied eagerness for regnant recognition on January 4th, 1995--a month and a half before his cancer started being felt:

Dear Self, I would so much like to write a letter, but to whom? So I guess I will write to you. How are you doing? No, really, I want to know. I guess I'm happy because I'm living as I believe, and what I believe I believe is good. If I could only look down and see where or if and to what extent my thoughts and influence is being carried through and into the lives of others. But I guess I can't know. Oh, so sad[063].

Later that month, he wrote, "Oh God, you are my God, and I want to love you today and forever with my whole mind and soul and body. And I want your love to pour through me to all people, in principle and in practice. Your will be done. I will go to work tomorrow and try to be logical and reasonable and alive[065]."

Six months later, during his chemotherapy treatments, Marty wrote, "Dear Father, I can't wait to die. Please use me[068]."

On November 12th, 1995, after his cancer remission, he lamented, "I can never write something so great as what just studying the Bible together can accomplish. So, as I reflect on this--I hate life. Why is everyone so braindead?[070]"

Two weeks later, he wrote, "'[W]ho wants to be a friend to such a depressing person?' I'm not trying to seek my own pleasure and happiness. I'm just trying to be reasonably wise as I try to keep from killing myself so I can try to be productive for the good of the world[075]."

On January 11th, 1996, Marty wrote, "I am trying to change the world from a bad and fearful one into a good and trusting one--that is the goal. Be wise, be reasonable; don't expect a reward...[078]"

Nine days later, he wrote, "I just wanna know the truth and we don't know the truth yet--how come no one cares? It's just a mess. I'm sorry. I don't know what to do[080]."

On March 3rd, 1996, Marty wrote, "Dear God, I don't know what to do for you. Do I really have nothing to contribute? I guess Le Mars doesn't want me... But where would I go?[084]" And a month and a half later, he wrote, "I do not know what the future holds for my small maladjusted life[089]."

Marty wondered, on June 7th, 1996, if it was possible for him to "justify trying to be a storywriter focusing mainly on that theme: girls[093]."

Parents' barn, with niece (vita age 8, bio age 28)

Marty told a co-worker on December 30th, 2000 that his self-appointed avocation was "[t]o avoid having a spurious spirit[104]."

During the summer of 2007, either in Cedar Falls or in Le Mars, Marty "jestfully" contemplated:

I don't know the animal code (laws). I know the divine code (laws). I don't know how to learn the animal laws. It's not something people teach. You're just supposed to DO IT. Do what's natural. I guess it depends on one's nature; whether one is an animal or a god. (Haha.)[110]

YouTube thumbnails (vita age 33)

One 2007 thought that he definitely had in Cedar Falls, probably while sitting on the third floor of the University of Northern Iowa library, was this:

Apparently girls or college girls must be taught, or just do it by instinct, to go in front of a boy or man if their body says they might be interested or attracted to him, and they stop for 1 or 2 or 3 seconds, and give him a chance to look only that long before making a decision to approach or not approach, as she tries to hook him (like a hooker). I don't think men can think that fast. I certainly can't think intelligently that fast. I don't know if other men, boys can think that fast or not. Maybe with practice. But I don't think it can really be called 'intelligent' thinking. Maybe 'penis' thinking, which is not intelligent thinking according to my definition[111].

Marty has struggled for decades to come up with the best--truthful and prudent--responses to the greeting, "How are you?" He has come up with some good responses and some bad ones. Perhaps, the best, vague,

meaningful even if ambiguous, response is: Just fair[114].
It's how he is and it's what he's trying to be.

He doesn't know how much longer he has to live--
perhaps a month, perhaps 50 years, perhaps some
amount of time in between these extremes. Has he
figured out his VRIO yet?[124] Maybe he has, maybe he
hasn't.

YouTube thumbnails (vita age 33)

Is some higher power trying to use him for something
good? Maybe yes, maybe no. Is *Sex with Jesus* the
vehicle to propel him, and others, to accomplish living a
life worth living? This remains to be seen. One thing
Marty has confessed is that "the more interest I can
generate in the words of Jesus and the life of Jesus and
the stock of Jesus, the higher the value of my investment
in Jesus[128]." Conservative Christians love to highlight
the facts and the murder (death) of Jesus. Marty,
alternatively, prefers to highlight the ideas and the life of
Jesus. Life, life, life. "He is not the God of the dead, but
of the living: ye do greatly err" (St. Mark 12:27, ASV,
public domain).

YouTube thumbnails (vita age 33)

SELF-ACTUALIZATION

As mentioned previously, Marty has had a difficult time pretending that the Philippine Islands experience did not affect the trajectory of his life[011]. That may, or may not, be an accurate surmise, but, either way, Marty expressed, on June 24th, 1989: "Thanks, God, for creating me to be who I am[008]."

So far his career prediction has primarily turned out to be a realization of his January 23rd, 1992 statement, when he said, "I'm never getting a real job, not unless it's artistic... [n]ot unless it's literary or musical[022]."

In 1992, he wrote, "[T]here are so many good books out. What can I contribute with my writings? Well, I'm not sure, but they haven't turned the world around and I know I can so I'm gonna do it[028]." Earlier that year, he had written, "To change the way people think. To begin to change the way people live... A masterpiece. The book of the century. By openly and fully pouring out my heart...[023]" Thirty years ago, he was not aware of the title yet: *Sex with Jesus*.

On August 17th, 1992, he wrote, "I gotta write a screenplay for Craig & Joan[026]." This is something he was able to accomplish (though he hasn't found financing for its production yet). Its writing, and its publication, has not yet had any noticeable effect upon the world's understanding (or sympathy) for suicidal thoughts, wishes, attempts, or successes[076].

On April 30th, 1996, after a cancer follow-up appointment, Marty wrote:

I'm staying with you. If you make my body scream, leave it deformed and ugly, or even take my body away, my soul is yours to the end. I want it to be true. I want to be strong... Dear God, please be gentle with me. Nothing too traumatic, until the final blow, of course[091].

Without regard to his sister's deterrence, one convention that Marty pushed beyond the limits of relates to the survey portion of *Sex with Jesus*, which he initially outlined as one of his first 2010 Milwaukee apartment projects, then set on the back burner until 2022. This project is aimed, among other things, toward recouping a legitimate definition of "love" that is not misinforming nor intended to dupe others[100].

On October 13th, 1993, Marty expressed his intention to "be a writer, a revolutionary, and a saint[044]."

Three months later, a work customer told him, "You're still young, you can do it[048]."

Perhaps, *Sex with Jesus*, along with the surveys, has shown that Marty will (be a writer), is (a revolutionary), can (be a saint), and has (written the truth).

In fulfillment of his desire to write truthfully, again, in February 1994, Marty wrote, "Maybe I should just start writing. Give me a month, two months, three months, and maybe I can 'concretize' what I want to say. Can I be motivated? We'll see[052]." It took around ten months, but, 29 years later, he finally got *Sex with Jesus* down on paper.

Sex with Jesus fulfills many of Marty's wishes, not the least of which was his April 8th, 2017 wish to coherently describe "the interrelationships among God, nature, and the world[134]."

Milwaukee living room (vita age 26)

On January 24th, 1996, Marty wrote, "Not anger. Not sadness. More so just a renewed conviction to keep pressing on, with pride (in the name of love)... and quietly[081]."

In hopes that it can be useful, Marty finally started creating the "sexual surveys as part of an 'industry-breaking' sex creation[130]" during the spring of 2022, mostly in Milwaukee, with a little work done at his parents' house in Le Mars during visits.

Milwaukee living room (vita age 35)

Is it possible to be a radical writer? Or is writing only a form of talking, and talking is the opposite of doing, being, taking radical actions? On June 13th, 1993, a work customer of his insisted Marty wasn't a radical, "because if you're a radical you'd be out there! instead of in here. And I said, 'you're completely right. I'm working on it!![042]'" He's still working on it. Funds are still lacking.

Still trying to be wise, productive, and reasonable, Marty wrote these four attributes on Christmas Eve, 1998: "Honesty, Humility, Poverty, Chastity[095]." A case can be made that he is fulfilling all four of these quite well.

On March 30th, 1993, Marty speculated about removing himself from his hometown when he wrote, "I think my best bet is to live in poor housing (but not subsidized or low-income housing, just crummy and cheap) not in Harlem but right next to it on upper west side. [H]ow will I get there? I don't need a car once there, but how will I get there?[035]" Marty landed in Milwaukee rather than in New York City, but he's carless, living in fairly frugal, unsubsidized housing. Looks like he's living the dream.

To get at the truth, the thing to do, and the thing he did, was to create (and copyright) the sex surveys (such as What Are You Like?[119]) using Likert scales, etc. The best way to get people to take them, and to answer them truthfully, is still being evaluated.

On January 12th, 1994, Marty put "together a small bulletin board to take with me when I move[046]." He used it as a small incentive to move out of his hometown environment (which he finally did 15-1/2 years later). It is sitting in the windowsill of his Milwaukee apartment bedroom.

Milwaukee apartment bedroom

On August 31st, 1992, Marty made a copy of a newspaper writing on *Our Town*--"it's now in my billfold and I think it'll stay[029]." It has. It's a story, in part, about a girl's flashback to her 12th birthday: "Do any human beings ever realize life while they live it?-- every, every minute?" "No... The saints and poets, maybe--they do some." A writing about girls. *Sex with Jesus* is also a writing about girls, as Marty has continued to focus on an aspect of living that has been insufficiently examined and explained. No longer.

To help Marty in his task of truthfulness--avoiding spuriousness--he legally changed his middle name to Spiritfair in March 2003, after having the idea to do so just after Valentine's Day in 2001[105].

Again, it's possible that some of Marty's desire to do great things through God were influenced by the formative Philippine trip[011]. Some of these great dreams he tried to fashion (as mission statements, etc.) in the summer of 2010, shortly before he moved from Iowa to Wisconsin[125].

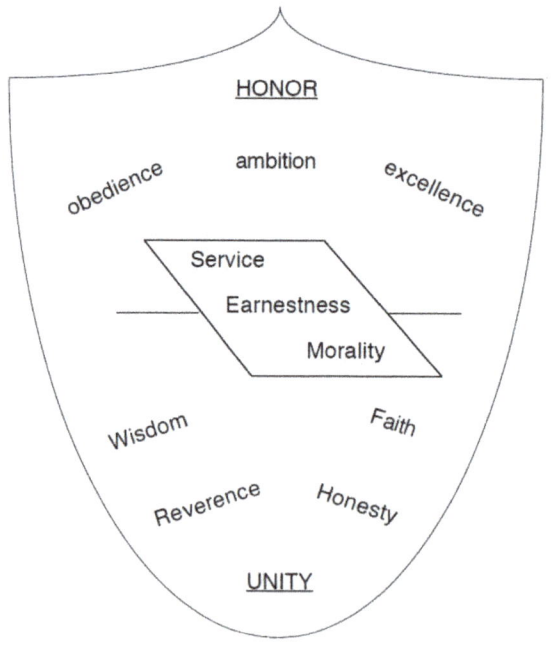

Mike Marty (created September 6, 2010)

If Mike Spiritfair Marty really had no remaining desires in his life other than to "change the world for Jesus[015]," it is logical that he would eventually need to move away from his hometown to expand his reach[064]. He did so in 2007, and he finally landed in Milwaukee, Wisconsin in the autumn of 2010.

Most serious people are probably pragmatic, i.e. they are just faking it for appearance's sake. Marty has always favored seriousness for some reason, though not necessarily for a pragmatic one. As he once wrote, "I want to talk, talk, talk about things that matter, matter, matter[079]." His writings have allowed him to maintain his serious bent.

Wanting to be an influencer of people[017], his first "serious" foray into doing so lasted a mere month before ennui began to encroach[017].

Nonplussed, that same month he howled at a friend more from conviction than from foresight, "I'm going to change the world or shoot two bullets through my head[016]."

Seeing problems in the world setup[088], Marty time and again has had to get back on track[032] when his way had become derailed.

A definition and understanding of the meaning of (agape) love[014] was seen by Marty as a necessary prerequisite for his version (and vision) of "progress." The importance of definitions first came to his awareness in April 1989, perhaps, when he was invited by an AOπ friend to help one of her sisters with a religion class question concerning the "kingdom of

God[006]."

When Marty told his roommate on October 9th, 1991 that he "was gonna change the world--no ifs, ands, or buts about it[018]," and that he wouldn't "conform to the world[012]," finally he has made true on that prophecy (over 30 years later) with his most recent metaphysical[126] achievement[123]--a credible, modern metaphysical system[098].

YouTube thumbnails (vita age 33)

Do rich people ever believe in metaphysical systems? No, they don't (even if they think they do, or they say they do, or they pretend they do). It's not possible for people who have money to believe in anything except their money. Machines do not need a real reason to live, nor do the small percentage of people who have plenty of discretionary income, but everyone else does need one.

It's difficult for people who have plenty of discretionary income to understand that if a person's only reason to live is to be a good consumer of products like milk and toilet paper--for the economy's sake--this is not a real reason to live. Not having a reason to live makes getting out of bed in the morning difficult. Thus, people who aren't asset-rich need metaphysical systems. Lying, as a metaphysical system, is unsustainable.

Marty's former anger[027] turned to action when, upon his mother's recent death, he failed to meet the false, empty, worldly requirements of the end of her life, but he has reinvigorated her memory as part of his new world fulfillment[131] (exemplifying a better understanding of what family is and means).

YouTube thumbnails (vita age 33)

Is the world able to be changed in a particular direction by people who declare it to be done[034]? It is. When a new idea, or a new expression of an idea, is brought into a decomposing culture[118], change will happen. In what direction will the change be? That is up to us.

Around June 27th, 1989, in his Iowa State fraternity summer "Beachview" room, Marty began seriously thinking[010] about metaphysical problem-solving. Has *Sex with Jesus* solved all of Earth's metaphysical (and mental) problems[098]? No, it hasn't, but it is one small step.

DEATH FULFILLMENT

Is Marty dead? Is Marty alive? As most people would agree, it's extraordinarily difficult to prove one's existence (whether one exists or does not exist).

Supposing that Marty is "still" alive, what does that mean? Vitalogically, he committed a suicide of the ego in 1987 when he became born again, when trying to fulfill all of the ego's wants and demands did not strike him as being "ultimately" worth the effort. He was reading through the gospels during his spare time when he wasn't studying. His dad was three miles away at Hawthorn Court on a six-month sabbatical. (Did Jeffrey Dahmer really live at that same Hawthorn Court in the mid-1960s when Dahmer's dad was working on a Ph.D. program? That is so weird; even more so now that Marty is living in Milwaukee.) And Marty's possible born again "day"--October 21st, 1987--was two days after the Black Monday market crash.

Iowa State University (bio age 19,
born again 3 months later--vita age 0)

With a dead ego and a living body (including Freud's id), how does one "live"? (LOL--Marty's still trying to figure that one out.) In 2020, he had the speculative thought that "the afterlife..." could theoretically mean "what happens (in your life) after you <u>die</u> and are born <u>again</u>, in this life, on earth..."

This could compose well with Emerson's *Wealth* essay idea about being thrifty so that one has the means to invest in the "higher laboratories, imagery and thought... courage and endurance... this is capital doubled, quadrupled, centupled... in spiritual creation..."

As Becker relates in *The Denial of Death*:

If you are the average man you give your heroic gift to the society in which you live, and you give the gift that society specifies in advance. If you are an artist you fashion a peculiarly personal gift, the justification of your own heroic identity, which means that it is always aimed at least partly over the heads of your fellow men.

Marty's final chapter has not yet been written (as far as he knows). It remains to be seen how it all unfolds.

APPENDIX

001-(7-30-1985) received first blowjob

July 30   Also first B J.
   I took Melanie to O'Garrity's + bought
my first sport coat. It was our 2 month
July 31   anniversary.
   The day after Melanie + I's 2 month
anniversary started well. I went over

[Return to Sex Fulfillments](#)

002-(9-2-1985) almost had sex

Sept. 2
   Went to Cassel's early to help fix
breakfast for their 30th wedding anniversary.
Then bummed on to or houses during the
day. Tried to help her with Algebra. Had
an experience (almost!) in my bedroom. Went
to football. Matt's competing with me for

[Return to Sex Fulfillments](#)

003-(9-27-1985) Ripped up a $200
004-(9-27-1985) leave alone, kill myself

Ordered Mel's flower. Didn't win duke.
Too bad. I could have worn the title
well. Realized how immature 18 year olds
are again. Ripped up a $200 award.
Whatever. I like myself. Everyone thinks
I'm too quiet. Well, I'm going to stay that
way. We won our 1B game against S.C. West
11-14. Now I'm going to break up with
Mel, definitely, the next time I talk to
her or see her. If I had any guts
what-so-ever, I would kill myself. I
wish everyone would just leave me
ALONE. I was keeping going with you
halfly because it was great going with a
popular girl, & halfly because I hoped you'd
change. You haven't & at this rate, won't.

Return to Active Efforts to Change World
Return to Death Wants

005-(4-15-1989) I started to realize

obstacle course at 10 & the 3-legged
race at 11. Then dinner. Then I got
depressed. But I started to realize as I
would much more strongly later in the day
that I am a loner. That's who I am &
I can do it & enjoy it. I get depressed
when I try to be who I am not. I

Return to Born

006-(4-26-1989) Helped Denise

from 4-4:30'. Judged Augmented Fifths at 7 — they're incredible. Helped Denise, the AOπ, w/ her Religion 221 question about the Kingdom of God.

Return to New World

007-(5-19-1989) I've really got to figure

Golfed this afternoon @ Homewood w/ Keno, Stu, & Krummen—shot a 56. Thought a lot about Kathy & Vicki today—Kathy left for California this morning. I told Keno I was sick of looking at girls after he told me to look at a couple of them. I've really got to figure out who I am this summer, my goals, & how I can achieve them. It was a fun day.

Return to Sex Fulfillments

008-(6-24-1989) Thanks God

12:30 over. Thanks God for creating me to be who I am, to

Return to Self-Actualization

009-(6-26-1989) Decided to do

accepted Jesus before). Decided to do my
3rd speech on monitoring depression. 30)

Return to Active Efforts to Change World

010-(6-27-1989) [started thinking

Bible study was fun talking about who are Christians
+ who are going to hell w/ Lori + Heidi + Terry
(for a while). Terry + I gabbed some in my room
after I picked her up from the pool + then I
fell asleep on the floor while she was still
studying. 30

this is when i
started thinking +
asking questions

Return to Counter Culture
Return to New World

011-(11-6-1989) I called M & D

I called M & D tonight + told them thanks
for the Philippines plus. I've said before
that I was definitely a different person
before + after the Philippines. I changed
a lot from 4th to 6th grade — I didn't
have to, but I was given the opportunity
to change into a guy who would do a lot of
things not according to the norm, + I did.
That was a poor, poor sentence. Thanks God
for letting me be me. I want you to do great
things through me if it be your will. Just +

Return to Born
Return to Self-Actualization

012-(11-7-1989) willing to be "un"normal

know, but God has given me the chance &
ability to be crazy, & I'm gonna take advantage
of it for his sake. God, I won't conform to
the world !! I'm gonna commit my life to doing your
will & if I do crazy things in the process, I
am more than willing. Maybe I can even check on

Return to Active Efforts to Change World
Return to New World

013-(11-18-1989) Did I place [excellence]

about the conversation afterwards led me
to think about my priorities again. Did I place
too much emphasis directly on God instead of
focusing my God-given talents toward excellence
while always focusing indirectly on God? Is that
compromising? I'll keep struggling. Earlier as

Return to Self-Knowledge

014-(12-23-1990) I decided last [the best]

"Freedom" single alot. the last couple of days. [I decided
last night that I am going to commit myself to being
...

* | the best teacher of agape love in the world. I
want to be the best. I I should start writing my

Return to Active Efforts to Change World
Return to New World

015-(8-29-1991) I have no desire

going. I have no desire before I die to do anything except
change the world for Jesus. Class was good today again. 30
Aug. 30 - Fri

Return to Feelings
Return to New World

016-(9-21-1991) I told her

to her it all, especially over the phone. I hate phones. I
told her I'm going to change the world or shoot two bullets
through my head, & I probably shouldn't have said that. When
I can't even see her eyes & she can't see mine or my smile,
it really doesn't mean the same thing as if we were talking in
person. She is right though, I shouldn't get so intense that I
get to a point where I do feel I have to kill myself, I just
have to keep on the simple path I'm on now & continue to learn &
continue to love! And pray, pray, pray. And be at peace.

Return to New World

52

017-(8/20 to 9/26/1991) be trustworthy, be with you

8-20-91   Be trustworthy.

8-22-91   Life goes on. Gotta keep trying to make as much of an impact as possible.

8-29-91   I have no desire before I die to do anything except change the world for Jesus.

9-12-91   If you say you're a Christian, then act like one.

~~~~~~ 9-26-91   God, I'm ready to be w/ you.

Return to New World

018-(10-9-1991) Norm and I

before work. Norm + I finished the book + then I went crazy + told him I was gonna change the world – no ifs, +s, or buts about it.   30   (we'll see – doubtful, haha)
Oct. 10 – Thurs.

Return to Active Efforts to Change World
Return to New World

019-(10-17-1991) My name is

My name is Michael Scott Marfy, I am 23 years old, & I am ready to die. I wouldn't mind living for another five or twenty or seventy years. I'd love to get married + raise some kids, I'd love to experience even more of the joys of life like family + friends + nature, but I'm not scared of death. My short time on earth has been complete. ~~~~~~~~~~~~~~~. ~~~~~~~~~~~~~. I've experienced success & I've lived through pain. ~~~ I've experienced the ecstasy of being alive. ~~~~~~~~~~ I'm ready to leave this earthly realm whenever that time might come.

Return to Self-Knowledge

020-(10-25-1991) Lord, I want to

lately. They were nice + they musta thought I was gorgeous or something by the looks in their eyes. Lord, I want to lead this generation. But you already knew that. And that one girl at P.H., the tall one w/ the

Return to Self-Knowledge

021-(10-31-1991) I got called in

for an all-night recording session. Oh, I got called in to work today at 11 + worked 11:30 - 7 + made 32 deliveries in the freezing rain + only fell twice. Including the fence I broke outside of our apartment yesterday, that makes 3. Norm says if he didn't know any better he'd think I was in love. Well, I think I am. W/o a doubt.

Return to Sex Wants

022-(1-23-1992) never getting a real job

something about getting a real job + I said, "I'm never getting a real job, not unless its artistic."

And Karen said "What?" And I said "Not unless its literary or musical." And Kolbeck said, "Or

Return to Self-Actualization

023-(3-15-1992) A masterpiece [book of the last 500 years]

To change the way people think. To begin to change the way people live. I can't spread the truth out among several volumes, that's too much like Kozd's descriptions of research. A masterpiece. The book of the century. By openly & fully pouring out my heart,

Return to Self-Actualization

024-(7-17-1992) I wanted to lead

And I thought how much I wanted to lead these youths out of pettinesses & into a love of the truth — which is a pure love for God & for all of mankind.

Return to Self-Knowledge

025-(8-15-1992) the No Better

I do not want the No Better Place to continue to be a place where we have fun & then have to struggle to get serious. NOT. It must be an atmosphere of seriousness & hard realities & diligent attempts to grapple w/ them. Also, Steve suggested (when we

Return to Feelings

026-(8-17-1992) I gotta write

for my absence at the wedding. I gotta write a screenplay for Craig + Joan. It could even be a musical. That would be way powerful. Mr. Susmihl

Return to Self-Actualization

027-(8-21-1992) And I am angry

showed Steve the anger inside me. And I am angry. Very angry. Mostly at Christians (or should I say "Christians") who live in various states of uncontested hypocrisy. When I got home, I wrote

Return to Counter Culture
Return to New World

028-(8-21-1992) man, there are

"Man, there are so many good books out. what can I contribute w/ my writings. well, i'm not sure, but they haven't turned the world around & I know I can. So I'm gonna do it." Then the

Return to Self-Actualization

029-(8-31-1992) Harvey Kluckh.

Then I went to Destmar (first, I made a copy of a Harvey Kluckhohn writing on "Our Town" its new in my billfold & I think it'll stay) &

Return to Self-Actualization

030-(10-1-1992) the old, old mower

path through the pasture & learned a very important
lesson. When I tried to start the old, old mower
I got mad 'cause it would not start & then it
would start & then stop. And I got really mad,
& even primal screamed one time. And then I
remembered. I really should have prayed & asked
for God's assistance beforehand. Father, you really,
really like to be included in everything don't
you — our jealous Lord. And after I prayed,
it never died again (is that right?) — I think it
started that very next time & ran wonderfully. The
path is fun. While I was mowing it, I basked in
the amazement of that relearned lesson, & in the

Return to Feelings

031-(12-13-1992) If they're cancer

those two lumpy bumps on my left side really kind of
bum me out. What are they? If they're certain cancer,
what am I gonna do? If they're just bumps that keep
being very tender when I touch them, then I guess
it's just a physical burden that I must bear along w/
all my spiritual ones. Maybe it's to constantly remind
me of the physical pain of others so I can relate.
I must press on. I hope it's not cancer. Father,
your will be done. Only let me love. Helped a lady

Return to Self-Knowledge

032-(1-5-1993) back on the track

finally, thankfully, got back on the track of my
dream... to change the world powerfully, while
living on the edge in the hands of God. I

Return to New World

57

033-(2-17-1993) push beyond

blowing, weather to mail 3 letters. You don't
know what you can do until you try it. Until
you push yourself beyond the limits of conventional
acceptability. Whatever that is! Amy called. Dad

Return to Self-Knowledge

034-(3-29-1993) Amy was really

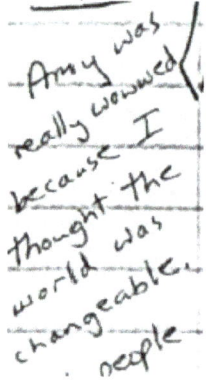

Amy was really wowwed I because the thought was world changeable. people

Return to Counter Culture
Return to New World

035-(3-30-1993) I think my best

I think my best bet is to live in poor
housing (but not subsidized or low income housing,
just crummy & cheap) not in Harlem but right
next to it on upper west side.

how will I get there?
I don't need a car once there, but how
will I get there?

Return to Self-Actualization

036-(5-30-1993) Thank you, Jesus

quite a while to Christy. Thank you, Jesus.
[Let me shine powerful alternative, truth-filled,
beams!!

Return to Feelings

037-(5-31-1993) did the big M

did the
big M, v it
was weird-
looking in a
Sears catalog
in the hall way

Return to Sex Wants
Return to Sex Fulfillments

038-(6-3-1993) Before the Philippines

'on' sexuality. "Before the Philippines I was "normal" sexually - chasing the girls + looking up their skirts, etc... I guess when we were in 1st or 2nd grade, & Stacy Thoms tried to kiss all the boys, I didn't like it too much (maybe), but I think that was pretty normal for that age too. When I came back from the Philippines I was still normal, but shy. Shy, not so much specifically sexually, but in all things. I didn't want to brag. From all I can scrounge out of my mind, I believe that is the simple truth. In 7th grade, I liked girls but I was shy. In eighth grade I liked girls but I didn't really like Jackie Gorrell all that much, & I was still shy. In ninth grade. I liked girls, I really did like Laura Doorenbos quite a bit, I did have a good time dancing w/ her at that one dance, but I was still very nerdy + shy. And I never did like that one joke

Laura told while us two + Hoang. (on his moped) were walking west on 12th St. toward my house. In 10th grade I too liked girls, but I was an absolute nerd. Thought I could be cool still hanging around Mayrose, but w/o having to go out on a scary date. Went to TWIRP w/ Marla. It wasn't very exciting. (Went to TWIRP in 9th grade w/ Shelly — I was very shy.) In 11th grade I met Melanie, & got to know her better, + the excitement of that relationship lasted halfway through my junior year in college. W/ Melanie I had fun making out, but I also just loved being w/ her & relating w/ her. In college I had my various crushes, mostly w/ Kathy Nutt. My 4th year I was pretty spiritual + under control working at Lemstone. I had a riot going up to the Michael W. Smith concert in Minneapolis in ~~Aug~~ October '89 w/ Kathy Nutt + others. During the summers, '88 - '90, I got my sexual allottment by working at the Ames pools. In my fifth year I was breaking out of my rigid Jesus freak mode, & Kathy Nutt was gone, & I really just did like girls but I didn't know how to approach them. The passion + the pain. Oh, student teaching at Boone, I really liked the girls, but I was pretty much under control too. From summer of '91, at home in LeMars + then in Ankeny + then at home again through I suppose ~~Febru~~ February or so of this year ('93) I was pretty under control, working w/ passion on a 'cause for Jesus. I was not gay, but just very spiritual as themes along those lines were mostly what I had in my mind. Then I suppose what broke me mostly out of it was the MWS concert w/ Tanya + then the 5-day later vocal f concert + then seeing her picture winning the high jump in the paper — I was intensely amazed by that. And then it was in April or May when I thought for the first time most seriously about the possibility of staying in LeMars for another 4 (?) years — paying off completely my college debt too, + writing my/our one book in the comfort + strength of a familiar home. And writing the script too.

like now?

11-26-97 And maybe leaving when I'm 29, nearly 30. And helping actually to turn LeMars + area upside down. This got me thinking again about how much harder it would be to resist being tied down to some local girl. I really don't think there's any chance it could ever happen, but there's that huge temptation of mine to dream. Then in the last couple of days, Monday + Tuesday I guess, my sexual throttle was running at full speed, thinking some of Tanya + looking at that one picture in the Sears catalog + thinking other thoughts. I'm not gay. It's nice to know. I want to be a man for Jesus!!!!! I just got an

add this to IDEAS, to Team notes, +
to Pulitzer bio (4-25-2023):

1. I think my emotional exhilaration
peaked pre-puberty at age 10 in
the Philippines helping to win the
Silliman BB championship (4th, 5th, 6th),
etc. (1978)(November?)

2. I think at the 6th-grade Sioux
Falls BB tourney, changing clothes in
a bathroom (not a locker room), I
got an impression that my genitals
were not gigantic which I think
henceforth affected my life (&
perhaps made me dubious about
replicating my age 10 ~~et~~ emotional
exhilaration in ~~that~~ any "genitallatic"
way at any future time during the
remainder of my life & existence
on earth) (1980 March?)

thanks for the kiss 38 years ago--you're the only person I've ever kissed--
how "unnormal" is that? LOL

me
To: liebsackm@gmail.com

I think Wayne notified me when Bob (and maybe Phyllis) died, so here's a notice for you (and Dave).

https://www.rexwinkelfh.com/obituary/june-marty

Have a good weekend, Melanie.

Mike Spiritfair Marty
Press Release

📎 2 Attachments Download all
🛡 Attachments scanned, safe to open

 4 business card SWJ bot...
110 KB

 Bark.png
3 MB

Return to Born
Return to Sex Wants

039-(6-4-1993) decided I'm gonna

Finally jumped off the yucky bed & decided I'm gonna start sleeping on the floor. Wrote

Return to Sex Fulfillments

040-(6-5-1993) Writing is my

line : honest & strong exhortation. Writing is my gift. I can do it. I can write the book & C & J. It's hard, but it's the only creative outlet I know of for everything that's going on in my mind.
       June 6 - Sun

Return to Self-Knowledge

041-(6-10-1993) I also said

is definitely where things happen. I also said I wished people would encourage my dream more instead of wanting me to settle down in loserville. I told her I might not be going to New York for a while. I told her again, that I would never change my passion, after she kinda asked me this time, & she thought that was really cool & I think she believed me — absolutely trustworthy. We

Return to Counter Culture

042-(6-13-1993) John Kneip was

June 13 - Sun

John Kneip was in & returned my book. He tried to tell me I wasn't a radical. And he told me he was very disappointed in my book, he said I preached too much, & though it hurt some for a bit, he wasn't thoroughly convincing. He showed me a few lines in the book he said I shouldn't have written & he said I shouldn't have started out w/ "God" & he said I shouldn't have used 9 fake people/names — I told him people really like to criticize. As he was leaving he'd moved far to the kind end of the spectrum. He said I wrote in a radical way, but I wasn't a radical. Why? I said again. He finally answered "because if you're a radical you'd be out there! instead of in here." And I said "you're completely right. I'm working on it!!" He said "you can be the next Martin Luther King." And I responded w/ "That is my dream!!" It was good. [It is 5:30 AM

Return to Self-Actualization

043-(8-22-1993) Tammy asked

Aug 22 - Sun

Lloyd's 75 bday. He called twice. Tammy asked me out. I fudged around it — she said she had a boyfriend, & I brought that up, & I told her I was a Jesus freak & that I really didn't have time for girls. Once she believed me, she thought that was pretty cool. I might take the

Return to Sex Wants

044-(10-13-1993) I will be a writer

to 6 or so. I will be a writer, a revolutionary, & a saint.

Return to Self-Actualization

045-(12-9-1993) I've prayed like

Christians. I've prayed like this before — he didn't give me Kathy, he didn't let me go to New York & become our nation's spiritual leader (not yet). I prayed for several huge things that I hoped to accomplish before I martyred out at 37 or 38. Just wrote a

Return to Death Wants

046-(1-12-1994) a small bulletin

bday card. And then finished putting together a small bulletin board to take w/ me when I move. Was planning on going to the wrestling

Return to Self-Actualization

047-(1-14-1994) I told him

write about. I told him, "I just want to try & make the world a better place." And he said "there's nothing wrong w/ that." He made some

Return to Active Efforts to Change World

048-(1-25-1994) I eventually

levels in this country. Score!! I eventually told him I wanted to be a writer & I just wanted to write the truth & I was ready to die. I told him I was 26 & he said, " You're still young, you can do it. "

Return to Self-Actualization

049-(2-3-1994) Told him I

Meade's civics class, we just went to the library. Told him I wanted to be free & write the truth. I don't think he thought that was too weird. Now we're in Fenderson's

Return to Self-Knowledge

050-(2-6-1994) I am so miserable

Feb 6 - Sun
I am so miserable.

Return to Feelings

051-(2-18-1994) that's who I

John 15:8. John 15:14 - that's who I want my friends to be, those who seek to do Jesus' commands as I do. Exercised. Rearranged room.

Return to Self-Knowledge

052-(2-19-1994) Maybe I should
053-(2-19-1994) it's called

people to love &, "tomorrow." Maybe I should just start writing. Give me a month, two months, three months, + maybe I can "concretize" what I want to say. Can I be motivated? We'll see. Oh, also realized what the definition of all the happy people who make me sick is: it's called hedonism.

Return to Self-Actualization
Return to Acclimatization to Evil

054-(2-27-1994) Harmony w/in an evil

Feb. 27 - Sun

Up at 11:45. Harmony w/in an evil system is not harmony & it's not seeking first the kingdom of God. I feel so torn, but here

Return to Acclimatization to Evil

055-(7-1-1994) I'm ready to kill myself

July 1 - Fri

Worked + stayed late + did inventory. I'm ready to kill myself. I think it's about time. But

Return to Death Wants

056-(8-6-1994) I'm ready to be

I'm ready to be free. The world won't be changed.

Aug 7 - Sun

Return to Feelings

057-(8-8-1994) Several thoughts about

Aug 8 - Mon

Did nothing today. No motivation. Several thoughts about killing myself the last few days — the thoughts come, ya know. Had a wonderful serious talk w/ M + D

Return to Death Wants

058-(8-22-1994) Came home and
059-(8-22-1994) Came...enough

fonts <Came home & Thought "why should I live?" I don't enjoy it. Tried to write a suicide note but I'm not motivated enough.> Borrowed

Return to Death Wants

060-(11-9-1994) I'm giving up

Work was ok. Left an hour early! I'm giving up on my family. Got two weak/frustrating letters from Lynnae + Alan & it's just not worth it. My family is the human race.

Return to Sex Wants

70

061-(11-10-1994) It's not each

didn't fit in. It's not each other's
hurting words that are heartless. It's
M dance, it's the whole setup, it's the
world. Do you not get understand?
Nov. 11 - Fri

Return to Active Efforts to Change World

062-(11-17-1994) Told mom that I

Ange. Told Mom that I thought I was
ready to disown my family + take the human
race for my family. I warned her + prepared
her + told her not to take this in the wrong
way but then I told her about some of
Jesus' statements on family which I understood
more than the conventional wisdom of "the
importance of family." Matt. 12:46-50 +
Matt 10:37, etc... And we talked + it was nice.
Thanks mom. I told her that it was the rest of
my external family I was disowning (including
Alan + Lynnae) more than her + dad. Pretty

Return to Sex Wants

063-(1-4-1995) Dear Self

Dear Self, I would so much like to write a letter, but to whom? So, I guess I will write to you. How are you doing? No, really, I want to know. I guess I'm happy because I'm living as I believe, + what I believe I believe is good. If I could only look down + see where or if + to what extent my thoughts + influence is being carried through + into the lives of others. But I guess I can't know. Oh so sad. But I guess I really do believe. G'night, mate.

Return to Self-Knowledge

064-(1-22-1995) I've beat on Le Mars

(maybe not! I've beat on LeMars enough. I've gotta have the strength to go for the world.)

turn in my next letter to the editor.

Return to New World

065-(1-29-1995) Oh, God, you are

of C + J accomplished. Oh God, you are my God, + I want to love you today + forever w/ my whole mind + soul + body. And I want your love to pour through me to all people, in principle + in practice. Your will be done. I will go to work tomorrow + try to be logical + reasonable + alive.

Return to Self-Knowledge

066-(4-14-1995) Thank you, Melanie

April 14 - Fri

Thank you, Melanie, for the 10-year anniversary of my first kiss to the only girl I will probably ever kiss. A

Return to Sex Fulfillments

067-(5-4-1995) I'd love to see

said. I love looking at naked women— boobs, butts, + vaginas/vulvas. I'd love to see naked or underwear-clad live versions of Angi Weiland, Mindy Conley, or Tanya Solma. But obviously, much, much rather I would like to be the national spiritual leader of my generation (+ beyond).

May 5 - Fri

Return to Sex Fulfillments

068-(7-19-1995) Dear Father

don't feel well but I think I'm past the vomit stage. I'll try to rest. Dear Father, I can't wait to die. Please use me.

Return to Self-Knowledge

73

069-(9-2-1995) A policeman

TEC, packed up, + headed out. A policeman stopped + asked me where I was going at such a late hour (about 3½ miles east of LeMars) + I told him everything save giving him a copy of CRIES. Finally, he said "ok," + I said "thank you, sir" + he drove off. Delivered 10 in Oyens — only a couple barking dogs. Then 39 in Remsen — a couple more barking dogs, but nothing major. Thank you, Father. Sat down a couple times in town + filled up some water at the Pronto outdoor faucet. Got to town at 1 + started heading home at 2. After just a few minutes I met 3 guys, from LeMars, whose car had broken down. I told them who I was after I'd said I was old (when they thought they might know me), but then one of the guys guessed (or kinda knew?) that I'd graduated in '86 or '87. It was kinda cool. 15 minutes later, 2 guys + 2 girls, stopped + I hopped in the back seat. My feet + legs weren't feeling terrible but not great either. We had a good talk. I told them what I was up to + they laughed some & ridiculed me (kindly) but I enjoyed it + I think they found it pretty darng interesting. They dropped me off at the

Depot at 2:35. I was in bed by 3.

Return to Active Efforts to Change World

070-(11-12-1995) I can never

I can never write something so great as what just studying the Bible together can accomplish. So, as I reflect on this — I hate life. Why is everyone so braindead?

Return to Self-Knowledge

74

071-(11-17-1995) I hate the world

won't. I hate the world. But it's where
I have to be. Felt like I was back

Return to Feelings

072-(11-24-1995) What exactly

What exactly is the emotion called which
I feel when I watch art of that
type? (It is now 2:15 pm on Saturday
+ we are at the hotel.) "Infectiousness" --
Leo's word is pretty good — when I get
infected by the love + beauty + truth
of the writer whose sympathies +
interests are akin to mine. Worked

Return to Feelings

073-(11-26-1995) I don't like the world

X I don't like the world. It's a
cruel haven. It's now after 5 pm

Return to Feelings

074-(11-26-1995) You can either

greed in the name of love, selfishness in
the name of love — that's America. "You
can either stay comfortable or have the
truth — you can't have both." That was

Return to Counter Culture

75

075-(11-28-1995) I'm just trying

because "who wants to be a friend to
such a depressing person?" I'm not
trying to seek my own pleasure or
happiness. I'm just trying to be reasonably
wise as I try to keep from killing
myself & so I can try to be productive
for the good of the world. While I

Return to Self-Knowledge

076-(11-30-1995) I am so damn

disappointed. I am so damn tired of no
one understanding the essence of suicide.
I've got to get back to the C & I
script (if I have the energy) — I've felt

it tugging at me a little lately. I

Return to Self-Actualization

077-(12-3-1995) Don't give up

Don't give up, don't give in, Marty. Keep pushing the limits. One day, just maybe,

someone will be able to love me & move me to full, unforced joy. Or else one day I'll die & then I can stop trying. World love. Dear Father, I'm yours, because it's a lot less tormenting that way.

Return to Feelings

77

078-(1-11-1996) I am trying to

I am trying to change the world from a

bad & fearful one into a good & trusting
one — that is the goal. Be wise, be
reasonable; don't expect a reward, but be
passionate for goodness. Create trouble.
Be wise. Think. Create trouble. Be
forgiving. Nay ta-ta! If I start being
abused for the truth this year or
next, is that to soon? No. Live today.
Be wise. Speak the truth. Expect no
reward, no outward show of thanks. The
truth remains the truth. Love one
another. Think. Be wise. Create
tension & be willing to suffer for it if
that is the will of God. Now I am

Return to Self-Knowledge

079-(1-20-1996) What should I do

cares. Amazing. What should I do? I
don't want to be silent for the rest of
my life. I want to talk, talk, talk
about things that matter, matter,
matter. What can I do? I can hardly

Return to New World

080-(1-20-1996) we don't know

pride. I just wanna know the truth & we don't know the truth yet — how come no one cares? It's just a mess. I'm sorry. I don't know what to do.

Jan 21 - Sun

081-(1-24-1996) Not anger

quiet inner fire mood. Not anger. Not sadness. More... just a renewed conviction to keep pressing on, w/ pride (in the name of love)... & quietly. Bought a

Return to Self-Actualization

082-(2-4-1996) Had a good

stop over for a bit. Had a good talk w/ Kathy but then it ended badly when we got to her house & ???? got started on a topic — suicide — which we weren't able to discuss adequately, so then it was just kinda left hanging & that's scary & seems bad but hopefully it will turn out good.

Feb 5 - Mon

Return to Failure

083-(2-25-1996) It's just not

'It's just not worth the effort.
Life, that is. Amazing. I'm sorry
but I'm just floored.' Early death
through martyrdom I guess, I must
not forget it. I guess this is just
God helping me to remember.>
  Feb 26 - Mon

Return to Death Wants

084-(3-3-1996) Dear God

new bldg. Napped. Did wash. Dear God,
'I don't know what to do for you. Do
I really have nothing to contribute? I
guess LeMars doesn't want me — it's Main
Street, ya know, + I'm just a
philosophizing Carol Kennicott. But where
would I go?' I don't know. I like

Return to Self-Knowledge

80

085-(3-9-1996) ...not so far

now. I am not happy. I had always
hoped to get the girl, but now that
seems quite beyond reach, & maybe not
even wise. I have nothing to live
for. Do I have a dream? Ha, what a
joke. It is still the same, but... Hm
Keep at it. Don't fret about the pretty
young lady. Don't fret about the desire
for love. Don't fret about my intellectual
isolation. I have friends, they're on my
shelves — I just don't have one to
hold. But still, the fact that I'm
paying back the debt (for the 1st 23
years) is not so far out of line.

Return to Sex Wants

81

086-(3-23-1996) spiritual whorehouse, Phaedo

3-23-96   The Church today is for people who are not too interested in spiritual things. For the spiritual seeker there needs to be continuous inspiration, not "same o, same o." Whatever. Anyway the church is for those people who give in too easily to a slanted + shallow answer to the meaning of it all. Each generation must ask the same questions as the previous one, but the church won't let them ask; + the church thinks that it is a believable entity, but it is not. It is a spiritual whorehouse where the members pay to be relieved at regular intervals from the burden of their meaningless lives.

< Joehh 13:12 >

A few pages into Plato's "Phaedo" I came across an argument against suicide which is more than anything in the whole Bible.

Return to Counter Culture

087-(3-24-1996) they are

they are contented to describe the world as it is + I want to describe how the kingdom of love should be.

Return to Feelings

088-(4-13-1996) How can I [excellence]

not get / something from that? Even in an occupational
id of / the people, way? I like excellence very much. How
but the / can I do something excellent to help
problems / eliminate (or reduce) the eyesores of our
that they / world? Hiding the eyesores isn't an
have talking / answer, it's a lie. How to get rid of
not like / them?, that is the question. I think love
● *Hitler here / is the answer. And wisdom. And goodness.*

Return to New World

089-(4-18-1996) I do not know

I do not know what the future holds
for my small maladjusted life.
    Apr 19 - Fri

Return to Self-Knowledge

090-(4-20-1996) Creative excellence [excellence]

last!! Pleasure is always followed
closely w/ pain. So what is the answer?
Creative truth. Creative love. Creative
excellence. Tonight was one of those

Return to Active Efforts to Change World

091-(4-30-1996) Dear God, please

me. I'm staying by you. If you make my body scream, leave it deformed & ugly, or even take my body away, my soul is yours to the end. I want it to be true. I want to be strong. I really shouldn't talk so much. Dear God, please be gentle w/ me. Nothing too traumatic, until the final blow, of course. I talk too much.

Return to Self-Actualization

092-(5-13-1996) I wish I

old bldg or by the little bridge. I wish I could solve the girl question & the life question, but I haven't been able to yet, & it's frustrating.

Return to Sex Wants

093-(6-7-1996) storywriter: girls

6-7-96   I was thinking about how I was maybe even to the point where I could justify trying to be a storywriter focusing mainly on <u>that</u> theme: girls. Chaste love & girls, I mean. It seems almost incompatible for me to want to continue to follow Jesus & serve God & also think & write about girls. But it seems like maybe it should be so. It's obviously a very important topic, & it's kind of subtly been my thing all along, & it's a very lost concept in our modern world.

Return to Self-Knowledge

094-(12-3-1997) vague idea

12-3-97 I have a vague idea in my head which I'd like to try & capture, even if it doesn't come out very clearly. I was reading through my diary entry during my cancer (3-16/17-95) when I wanted to be put to death but they wouldn't do it. Here's why, I believe. Business (which includes religion & health care) want lots of people, & they don't want people to go around being killed or especially killing themselves, because the more people, the more stupid people, the more unhealthy people, etc., the more these raw material bodies can contribute to the materialistic Gross National Product ~~www~~ &—since they're stupid & unhealthy—that much more of the money they earn will go to the businesses & churches & hospitals, etc. On the other hand, for those of us who feel the burden of helping all people to be healthy & wise, we would vote for <u>less</u> people rather than <u>more</u>. Because these business-minded people want <u>more</u> people, they also are hearty supporters

of a high birth rate as well as a low death rate. To mothers w/ new babies, they are the most common culprits to be heard saying, "Oh, isn't he/she cute!" And so on & so forth. (Including also the "mental health" profession.)

Return to Counter Culture

095-(12-24-1998) honesty, humility

12-24-98 Honesty, Humility, Poverty, Chastity

Return to Self-Actualization

096-(1-30-2000) control / kingdom

1-30-00

When people sometimes say "God is in control," what does this mean?

    1. Does it mean that people have no free will, that God controls our every thought & act?

  or 2. Does it mean that the world is just the way God wants it to be?

  or 3. Does it mean that God has control inasmuch as he won't let humankind destroy each other or the earth completely, but as long as we're not on the very brink of destruction, he lets us try to rule ourselves?

When people talk about "the kingdom of God," what do they mean?

    1. God someday will come down from heaven & create a heaven on earth by his own will & power

  or 2. Mankind is responsible by its own efforts to create a heaven on earth

  or 3. There is truly an afterlife, & when each person dies, he or she will hopefully go to heaven (i.e. he or she will "inherit" the kingdom of God)

  or 4. "The kingdom of God is within you" (Luke 17:21). And each man "will be a ruler in the city... which exists in idea only... & beholding, may take up his abode there. But whether such an one... ever will exist in fact, is no matter; for he will live after the manner of that city, having nothing to do w/ any other" (Plato's Republic. End of book IX.).

Return to Acclimatization to Evil

097-(4-11-2000) Death is non-being

4-11-00

Death is non-being for the individual. Doesn't that make more sense than an afterlife? That makes life more precious + our chance to seek God in this life. Our chance to seek "spiritual ecstasy" in this life (as Joe Valenta said). "He is not the God of the dead, but the God of the living" (Mark 12:27). Where life came from in the first place is still in question. "With God all things are possible" (Matthew 19:26). God is the possibility in this life. The possibility of the mind, of the spirit. This God is not the Creator of Nature + all of existence, this God is not He who is the master of evolution + the survival of the fittest, this God is not He who gives me a boner + a desire for the propagation of the species. This God is higher. He is the God of the possibility. Anything is possible, not in this world, but in my mind. (That sounds like dualism, which I've always been a little wary of. What is true?) Who knows? The worst hypocrites are all dualists. Righteousness still Rules!

Return to Counter Culture

098-(late spring 2000) Need to fabricate

Need to fabricate a believable modern metaphysical system to help us each get out of bed in the morning w/ a more noble impetus than money or fear + necessity — rediscovering metaphysical credibility

Return to New World

88

099-(early summer 2000) You ask me how I am

You ask me how I am. Why don't you tell me? What if I'm doing well. Isn't it bragging if fortune is smiling kindly on me? "Let another man praise you, & not your own mouth; A stranger, & not your own lips" (Proverbs 27:2). Am I kind? Am I boring? Am I cowardly? Am I beautiful? Do I give you pleasure? Do I make you uncomfortable? Do you like me? Do you love me? Am I sensitive to your moods, your joys, your pains? Am I unperceptive & cold? Why don't you tell me "how I am" & how I make you feel. Unless I make no impression on you whatsoever, in which case you probably don't care about me at all, so why pretend that you do by asking "how I am."

Return to Counter Culture

100-(7-16-2000) Lynnae, unencouragingly

7-16-00 "Dear is the like in virtue to the like, & the equal to the equal; dear also, though unlike, is he who has abundance to him who is in want. And when either of these friendships becomes excessive, we term the excess love" (PLA-59, Laws VIII). How does this description of love work as an ~~all bathing~~ overall definition of love (i.e. eros, philos, agape, etc.)? Male + female relationships (or perhaps also homosexual) are mostly eros + "dear, though unlike." When the feeling becomes "excessive," we call it love. That's easy to understand for it is the most common use of the term love in our culture today. Philos can be both like or unlike, equal or unequal. Agape is mostly found (if at all) in unlike + unequal relationships. Maybe for agape, we see "love" present if the tenderness + sincerity + compassion + selflessness is supernatural + "excessive <u>compared</u> <u>to</u> <u>the</u> <u>norm</u>" of how most humans would relate in a similar situation. For philos also, perhaps we call it love if the friendship is excessively intimate <u>compared</u> <u>to</u> <u>the</u> <u>norm</u>. This short treatment is my first serious attempt to bring the various forms of love under one all-encompassing definition (even though my sister, Lynnae, unencouragingly last Feb. said it couldn't be done).

Return to Self-Actualization

101-(8-17-2000) humanity's inborn nature

8-17-00 The confusion over humanity's inborn nature, whether we are born good or bad, whether we are supposed to do "what's natural" or resist our impulses, comes, in part, from verses like these: "we all once conducted ourselves in the lusts of our flesh, fulfilling the desires of the flesh & of the mind, & were by nature children of wrath" (Eph. 2:3); "their women exchanged the natural use for what is against nature. Likewise also the men, leaving the natural use of the woman, burned in their lust for one another" (Rom. 1:26-7); "His divine power has given to us all things that pertain to life & godliness... that through these you may be partakers of the divine nature, having escaped the corruption that is in the world through lust" (2 Pet. 1:3, 4). What is natural, what is given to us by nature, & are we to deviate (either "rise above" or "sink below") from this or "obey" it? Yes, marriage. Is marriage natural? Are you sure? You can quote Matthew 19:6 if you want, but are you sure the meaning is crystal clear, & do you really believe it? But more than just marriage. Natural or unnatural? Gray. It depends. I'd like to talk about it.

Return to Sex Wants

102-(9-9-2000) If I could ever

9-9-00   If I could ever touch a woman, while my income
(& erection) is yet small, maybe I would have
to think in terms of "working" to give the
woman pleasure during petting instead of
just showering expensive gifts on her to
seduce her beforehand. A line from "Don Juan
de Marco" ~~made~~ makes me think that maybe
this would be appealing to women. Also, I
remember, w/ Melanie, that petting can be hard
work + (at least for me) I often preferred the
moments when I just laid back & let her do
the work. "Work" & "money" are supposed

to be the same or related. If I don't
have enough money (or charm or pizzazz) to
impress beautiful ladies, maybe if I give
them my "work", they'd give me a chance.
Has "she" become my idol, dear LORD? I
know, I know, but where are ~~XXXX~~ You?
"I don't know how to love You... any better.
By loving "Her," would I also be loving You?
"He who does not love his [sister] whom he has
seen, how can he love God whom he has
not seen?" (1 John 4:20)   Does that apply
here?

Return to Sex Wants

103-(September 2000) Questions for Larry

Sept. '00   Questions for Larry Adler: Does God say the Bible is the perfect Truth; does the Bible say the Bible is the perfect, inerrant Truth? If God doesn't say the Bible is the Truth, how can we trust only fallible, sinful man to say that it is? If Jesus is the Word, + the Word is the Bible, + the Word is the Truth, + Jesus is the Truth, does this mean that Jesus is the Bible? How did the writers of the biblical books know that their writings were in-breathed by God + that the other writers at the time did not also write anything that was in-breathed by God? Did God tell them? Did any other witnesses hear these words of God?

Return to Counter Culture

104-(12-30-2000) no spurious spirit

12-30-00   Told Eric in a letter I had a task. What is it? To avoid having a spurious spirit.

Return to Self-Knowledge

105-(2-16-2001) change to Spiritfair

2-16-1   Michael Spiritfair Marty Should I change my middle initial S. (Scott) to something like this?

Return to Self-Actualization

106-(10-24-2005) yelled at M & D

Three of many reasons why I yelled at M & D
on 10-24-05 :
1. I don't like food being set in front of
   me which I haven't chosen — I like to
   choose what, & what amount, to eat when
   I am hungry
2. I don't want to hug or touch when I
   don't want to — I don't want Grandma to
   assume she can get a hug from me —
   maybe I don't want one (you have to
   ask)
3. I don't like seeing smiling faces on
   depressed people — the ultimate in
   schizophrenic behavior — the ultimate lie

Return to Feelings

107-(summer 2007) I want to bring Jesus

I want to bring Jesus into my sex life but
pretty women absolutely do not want
Jesus to be in their sex life — so there
is no connection nor even a possibility
of one

Return to Sex Wants

108-(summer 2007) I'm 39.

I'm 39. I discovered masturbation (usually using hard-core, sometimes soft-core, pornography, rarely nothing) at age 25 & it's worked pretty well for me - it's extremely efficient & it makes me feel happy. I left it at home hoping I could learn how to get along w/o it these 8 weeks, or else it would help motivate me to pursue actual woman contact. But I don't really like women. And if they got to know me I don't think they'd like me. I don't like pretending or manipulating, & I'm not sure that

I believe casual intercourse is good. Petting w/o ejaculation might be fun but I'm not sure if it would be satisfying or not. I think I should probably stick w/ pornography these next 8 weeks. Do you agree? Without it I will be unhappy & will not be able to concentrate on my studies. Any tips on connecting w/ women? I don't want to connect w/ a woman unless she wants to connect w/ me. How to know? No adult bookstores in town? Approaching a woman feels like selling my soul & dignity to her. So far I have been unable to reconcile it w/ my faith.

Return to Sex Fulfillments

109-(summer 2007) If anyone ever asks

if anyone ever asks me if I'm a virgin, be prepared to say: "I will tell you if you also will tell me the total # of times you have had sex in your life, w/ men, or w/ women, or w/ non-human animals."

Return to Counter Culture

110-(summer 2007) I don't know the animal

I don't know the animal code (laws). I know the divine code (laws). I don't know how to learn the animal laws. It's not something people teach. You're just supposed to DO IT. Do what's natural. I guess it depends on one's nature; whether one is an animal or a god. (Haha.)

Return to Self-Knowledge

111-(6-26-2007) chance to look for 2 seconds

6-26-07   Apparently girls or college girls must be taught, or just do it by instinct, to go in front of a boy or man if their body says they might be interested or attracted to him, + they stop for 1 or 2 or 3 seconds, + give him a chance to look only that long before making a decision to approach or not approach, as she tries to hook him (like a hooker). I don't think men can think that fast. I certainly can't think intelligently that fast. I don't know if other men, boys can think that fast or not. Maybe w/ practice. But I don't think it can really be called "intelligent" thinking. Maybe "penis" thinking, which is not intelligent thinking according to my definition.

Return to Self-Knowledge

112-(10-14-2007) epiphany growingness

an epiphany - 10-14-07 - contribute something new to planet - what's new? - aggressive to add something new + "valuable" in your field of expertise - progress - have I contributed anything new? Could I? Should I? What field? Not possible any longer? - growing like crystals into the void - planting excitingly + aggressively into women to continue ~~both the~~ the growingness - if I don't lead + contribute something new (instead of reworking + reminding the old as I have done), then I'm only biding time + serving the leaders - Why Peace Is Bad - Is Truth Bad? Is "Ich Du" satisfying or superficial? If it's satisfying, is it antiprogressive? - Should I pursue doctorate of philosophy at U of I, + then be a writer of simple truths to the people - not a professor - MBA first? yes - in order to be able to incorporate money into ~~#~~ my "new thing" - 3.0 MBA? - how do I make money? - graveyard production supervisor? - what about aggression + my penis?

- sex, truth, money - integrating them - is this also not new? - is women + men using each other + calling it love (which it isn't except in the animal sense) acceptable? - Do I want to produce something new, or do I want to make money so that I can be respectable + pursue women? I don't want to be enslaved to a career or a woman. I want to be free, but I also want to make money + pursue women. How ~~w~~ do? So that I can pursue women? - Is that my goal? - It's not much to live for? In fact, it's nothing. Emptiness.

That movie, Chasing Amy, maybe should have been called Chasing Emptiness, b/c that's what you're chasing when you're chasing Amy (both in a physical sense + a substantial sense).

Return to Sex Wants
Return to Sex Fulfillments

113-(2008?) the Latin

Does the Latin word "venus" (venal, venereal) mean "love" + "sale"? Do "love" + "sale" mean the same thing somehow or is that not accurate? Venereal: of sexual intercourse. Venal: open to, or characterized by, corruption or bribery.

Return to Acclimatization to Evil

114-('08, 6-8-11) Just fair.

How are you? Just fair.

Return to Self-Knowledge

115-(Jan. 2009?) talk about the dark

talk about the dark + my sex life searching for greater understanding — one hr a week for 8 wks (the purpose) this summer w/ UNI counselor

Return to Sex Wants

116-(8-3-2009) cross-fertilization

8-3-09 Does science say that cross-fertilization is good + religions generally do not support this? Is this the primary conflict b/t science + religion?

Return to Sex Wants

117-(fall 2009) what? does

what? does "fittest" (in "survival of the fittest")
mean alignment, fit, appropriate for achieving
some purpose, qualified, competent, instead of
meaning "healthiness" or "strength" ???
[strategy book, p. 432] or does it even more
specifically mean what suits "her" since her is
the one who carries out the selection process in
both sexual + nonsexual ways?? cf IDEAS, p. 308

Return to Acclimatization to Evil

118-(11-5-2009) "grow out of"

From discussion during last strategy class (Nov. 5, Guy Fawkes):
Culture is what you "grow out of"
e.g. agriculture, Aristotle, petri dish, biology, earth,
gaia
Plato, Jesus, revelation — bring something new into
culture
in order for an individual, organization, or society to
"choose" a culture (or behavior) change, seeing the
cliff, + being at the brink of a crisis, is typically
required
needs disconfirmation, + then confirmation of
alternative, for there to be a change in
values/assumptions
social psychology / social movements

Return to New World

119-(winter 2009-10) A "What Are

A "What Are You Like?" survey — would you fill out a
(confidential) what are you like survey for me?
— already on facebook or dating ~~websites~~ sites?
I can see what you look like, ~~bu~~ but what are
you like — more efficient — Likerts —
attributes (use some theory)(copyright it)

Return to Self-Actualization

120-(winter 2009-10) men perhaps

men perhaps like to publicize their sexual activities;
women sort of like to keep their sexual
activities darked; women's bust size is sort of
public information; men's erection dimensions
are sort of darked; men have one public &
one private; women have one public & one
private; to make information better, & to
lessen market failure, perhaps the way to
bring female sexual activity into public view,
we need to make men's erection dimensions
public as well — I'm a 5 1/4 ~~6~~ (length) — 4 3/4
(circumference)

Return to Counter Culture

121-(2-18-2010) there are almost

there are almost no restrictions or restraints or laws w/ respect to the most powerful power in the world — the feeling of intercourse or ejaculation — generally this is the power of women & it is unregulated — it is the problem of volatility which is worse than unregulated derivatives or hedges. Women have the greatest power in the world, & there are a couple of la-de-da laws but all of the power happens in the dark + the la-de-da laws do not reach into the dark (ineffective regulation) + only matter at all when matters come into the light (which is uncommon) ⟨2-18-10⟩ — write quantifiable scholarly article on this —

Return to Feelings

122-(3-21-2010) future slaves

wait a minute — Republicans are ~~totally~~ anti-abortion b/c they know that if poor, stupid people are allowed to have abortions, there won't be enough current + future slaves to do the required work to support the easy-going lives of the wealthy (3-21-10)

Return to Counter Culture

123-(spring 2010) spend the next

spend the next 20 years creating an academic mental framework reconciling the yin-yang + the cross w/ reality

Return to New World

124-(summer 2010) come up w/ my

come up w/ my VRIO that is valuable, rare, &
inimitable — organize it effectively &
intelligently — for sustainable competitive
advantage

Return to Self-Knowledge

125-(summer 2010) use Beta Gam Sig

use BΠΣ & FH oaths as part of mission?

Return to Self-Actualization

126-(7-29-2010) write Franc   [does SWJ do this?]

write Franc as a confession, w/ a logical thread &
alignment & destiny ideas — each page, each #
perfect & powerful to help the populace love
the truth (7-29-10) & strengthen America's &
the world's reason to live — give them a true
one — is there one? — has to include & be
respectable to extraverts, warriors, & Don Juans,
as well as the smart people & the stupid
people. ~ 100 pages? 400 paragraphs? quien sabe

Return to New World

127-(11-14-2010) sexual fundamentality

11-14-2010

cf IDEAS p. 146-7

Second, Foucault sees the modern concept of homosexuality arising from
a desire to see sexuality as a fundamental aspect of who we are. Before
the 19th century, sodomy was simply regarded as a criminal act. Since the
19th century, sodomy has been regarded as just one manifestation of a
person's homosexuality. "Homosexuality" ceased to be associated with
certain acts, and became associated with a person's identity, with his soul.
One's sexuality became a key to interpreting one's personality and one's
behavior. Rather than work to eliminate homosexual acts, the growing
discourse around homosexuality saw these acts as constitutive of a
person's identity.

Return to Feelings

128-(Nov. 2010) the more interest

the more interest I can generate in the words
of Jesus + the life of Jesus + the stock
of Jesus, the higher the value of my
investment in Jesus

Return to Self-Knowledge

129-(11-7-2010) will of a woman

11-7-10

Many men think the best way to be happy is to
do the will of a woman (as in The Princess Bride
"as you wish," Wayne Denzel Washington)

the question becomes: is doing the will of a woman the
same as doing the will of God?

if the will of a woman is to be a part of
women + the task of women is to judge +
seperate desirable men from undesirable men
in an evolutionary way, + to naturally select
the desirable men + not to select the
undesirable men, + if the will of God is justice
+ peace + truth in the holy spirit (cf Romans
14:17-18), does women's evolutionary judgment
result in justice + peace + truth in the holy
spirit?

make arguments for justice, peace, truth
examine if woman's judgment results in justice (it might or it might not)
" " " " " peace "
" " " " truth "
use this structure as basis for sex journal writing
MADE IN U.S.A
examine if holy spirit result?
too

AMERICAN

Return to Acclimatization to Evil

130-(2011?) use sexual surveys

use sexual surveys as part of an "& industry-breaking" sex creation? (from strategy book)

Return to Self-Actualization

131-(5-1-2012) June funeral

5-1-2012 family values is wrong: use "my family is do will of god" verse, "let dead bury dead" verse, "where i am there you will be also" verse, "born of flesh is flesh, born of spirit is spirit" verse, etc.

Return to New World

132-(2013?) is...anything

is there anything to the notion that Jesus died on Friday (according to what THEY tell us, LOL) & people TGIF (thank God it's Friday; cf IDEAS pp. 358, 359?) + Jesus was dead during the weekend (through Saturday) & people love weekends (cf John 3:19) + the feeling I have had & have that people do not want Jesus to have anything to do w/ their sex lives & the progression of the sexual righteousness surveys project (keep out!)? [that's not right-I haven't really done anything w/ the surveys yet including creating them, after the background material has been gathered-not sure that there will be any roadblocks, though I "feel" that there might be] balance again? private & public? yinyang again? who created the weekend & when? how universal is it (or not)? TGIF - Jesus Is Dead! (cf IDEAS, p. 253, etc, etc.)

Return to Sex Wants

133-(3-2-2014) not How are you?

"How are you?" is not a Christian question.
(3-2-2014) (is the question ever asked in
the NT? no? only in OT? Christians are
Christians b/c of suffering not b/c of
joyous happyhood, cf The Final movie)

Return to Counter Culture

134-(4-8-2017) God nature world [SWJ cogito]

do a definitive PhD dissertation on the
interrelationships among God, nature, + the
world (4-8-2017)

Return to Self-Actualization

Please provide an accurate, online review of your opinion of this book if possible. (Thanks, if you have. You can tell all your friends, too.)

www.youtube.com/@getajahb350/playlists